FOOTBALL

Wit

FOOTBALL WIT

First published in 2008
Reprinted 2009, 2010, 2011, 2012
This edition copyright © Summersdale Publishers Ltd, 2013

Illustrations © Ian Baker

Aubrey Malone has asserted his right to be identified as the author of this work in accordance with sections 77 and 78 of the Copyright, Designs and Patents Act 1988.

Summersdale Publishers Ltd
46 West Street
Chichester
West Sussex
PO19 1RP
UK

www.summersdale.com

Printed and bound by CPI Group (UK) Ltd, Croydon, CR0 4YY

ISBN: 978-1-84953-459-8

Substantial discounts on bulk quantities of Summersdale books are available to corporations, professional associations and other organisations. For details contact Nicky Douglas by telephone: +44 (0) 1243 756902, fax: +44 (0) 1243 786300 or email: nicky@summersdale.com.

FOOTBALL Wit

QUIPS AND QUOTES FOR THE FOOTBALL FANATIC

AUBREY MALONE

summersdale

CONTENTS

EDITOR'S NOTE

Football players aren't necessarily expected to be funny, or even articulate. As Brian Clough once noted, their brains are in their feet. Which means that when someone comes out with a thought-provoking comment, like for instance Eric Cantona's famous pronouncement on press intrusiveness ('When the seagulls follow the trawler, it is because they think sardines will be thrown into the sea'), people react almost as if they've just heard a latter-day Shakespeare.

A lot of the so-called wit in these pages is unwitting, if you'll forgive the contradiction. This is the football world's confused (and often confusing) meanderings on lame-duck managers, overpriced (and under-performing) stars, visually challenged referees and cash-hungry magnates. If you're an aficionado of *Match of the Day* you'll know what it's like to suffer dull post mortems. But occasionally a pundit comes out with a nugget – intentionally or otherwise – and it's up to anthologists like me to commit these to memory and regurgitate them for your delectation.

As the man said, football's a funny old game.

───────

CAN YOU MANAGE IT?

There's only one
certainty in football:
managers get sacked.

BRIAN KERR, IRISH FOOTBALL MANAGER

Steve McClaren has achieved
the unique feat of making even
Sven Goran-Eriksson look good.

IAN RIDLEY, AUSTRALIAN FOOTBALLER AND COACH

———•◉•———

There are two types of manager:
those who've just been sacked and
those who are just about to be.

HOWARD WILKINSON, ENGLISH FOOTBALLER AND MANAGER

———•◉•———

Barry Fry's management is
based on the chaos theory.

MARK MCGHEE, SCOTTISH FOOTBALLER AND MANAGER

For me to win the Manager of
the Month award I would have
to win nine games out of eight.

NEIL WARNOCK, FOOTBALL MANAGER

———•●•———

You're not a real manager
until you've been sacked.

MALCOLM ALLISON, 'BIG MAL', ENGLISH FOOTBALLER AND MANAGER

———•●•———

Even Ferguson and Wenger had
their recurrent weaknesses;
neither, to take a common
instance, appeared capable
of distinguishing a top-class
goalkeeper from a cheese
and tomato sandwich.

PATRICK BARCLAY, SCOTTISH SPORTSWRITER

Sir Alex Ferguson is the best
manager I've had at this level.
Well, he's the only manager
I've had at this level.

DAVID BECKHAM, ENGLISH FOOTBALLER

Arsene Wenger and Alex
Ferguson don't conduct post-match
pleasantries as a general rule. The
Arsenal manager would, however,
be happy to crack open a bottle of
red with his Manchester United
counterpart — provided he could
use the Scot's head as a corkscrew.

ANDREW FIFIELD, BRITISH SPORTSWRITER

If a manager isn't fired
with enthusiasm he'll be
fired — with enthusiasm.

JOE LOVEJOY, ENGLISH FOOTBALL WRITER

The easiest team for a manager to pick is the Hindsight Eleven.

CRAIG BROWN, SCOTTISH FOOTBALLER AND MANAGER

———◦●◦———

A manager must buy cheap and sell dear. If another manager rings to ask me about a player I'll say 'He's great, super lad, goes to church twice a day. Good in the air, two lovely feet, make a great son-in-law.' You never tell them he couldn't trap a bag of cement.

TOMMY DOCHERTY, SCOTTISH FOOTBALLER AND MANAGER

———◦●◦———

Chelsea have just launched a new aftershave called 'The Special One' by U Go Boss.

PAT FLANAGAN AFTER JOSÉ MOURINHO'S
SHOCK DEPARTURE FROM CHELSEA

Great leaders inspire their men to glory. Steve McClaren will be remembered as a wally with a brolly.

DAILY MAIL

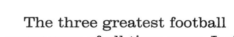

The three greatest football managers of all time were Jock Stein, Jock Stein and Jock Stein.

DOUG MCLEOD

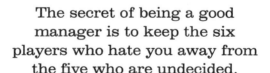

The secret of being a good manager is to keep the six players who hate you away from the five who are undecided.

JOCK STEIN, SCOTTISH FOOTBALLER AND MANAGER

If Mickey Mouse had taken charge,
it would have given the place a lift.

MIKE WALKER, WELSH FOOTBALLER AND MANAGER, ON EVERTON

———•●•———

I have come to the conclusion
that nice men do not make
the best managers.

GRAEME SOUNESS, SCOTTISH FOOTBALLER AND MANAGER

———•●•———

Matt Busby was the eternal
optimist. In 1968 he still believed
that Glenn Miller was just missing.

PATRICK CRERAND, SCOTTISH FOOTBALLER

IGNORANCE IS BLISS

When God gave Paul
Gascoigne his enormous
footballing talent, he
took his brain out
at the same time to
even things up.

TONY BANKS, BRITISH MUSICIAN

An oxymoron is when two
contradictory concepts
are juxtaposed, as in
'footballing brain'.

PATRICK MURRAY, ENGLISH ACTOR

———— ●●● ————

When I signed Jim Holton from
Shrewsbury for £100,000, Harry
Gregg told me I had a player
who didn't know the meaning
of the word defeat. I told him
defeat wasn't the only word he
didn't understand. There was
also pass, control, dribble...

TOMMY DOCHERTY

———— ●●● ————

He's got the brains of
a rocking horse.

DAVE BASSETT, ENGLISH FOOTBALLER AND MANAGER,
ON GOALKEEPER SIMON TRACEY

Jason Roberts? This is a man who spelt his name wrong on his transfer request.

GARY MEGSON, ENGLISH FOOTBALLER AND MANAGER

Ponderous as a carthorse and
slow-witted as a football donkey,
it's hardly Vinnie Jones's fault
that such a clodhopper – sorry,
former hod-carrier – has been able
to wrangle a prosperous living
from the professional game.

JEFF POWELL, BRITISH SPORTSWRITER

Slim Jim had everything
required of a great Scottish
footballer. Outrageously skilled,
totally irresponsible, supremely
arrogant and thick as mince.

ALASTAIR MCSPORRAN, SPORTSWRITER, ON
RANGERS PLAYER, JIM BAXTER

Dan Quayle thinks the Gaza Strip
is Paul Gascoigne's football jersey.

JOHNNY CARSON, AMERICAN TELEVISION HOST

The trouble with you, son, is that your brains are all in your head.

BILL SHANKLY, SCOTTISH FOOTBALLER AND MANAGER, TO ONE OF HIS PLAYERS WHO UNDERWHELMED HIM

———•◦•———

He's incredibly loyal. Ask him to jump off the stand roof and he'll do it. But he's as thick as two short planks. He always grabbed the quiz book on our coach trips so he could ask the questions. That way he didn't have to answer them.

ARNIE REED, PHYSIOTHERAPIST, ON VINNIE JONES

———•◦•———

Paul Gascoigne wore a Number 10 jersey. I thought that was his position, but it turned out it was his IQ.

GEORGE BEST, NORTHERN IRISH FOOTBALLER

The match will be shown on
Match of the Day this evening.
If you don't want to know the
result, look away now as we
show you Tony Adams lifting
the trophy for Arsenal.

STEVE RIDER, ENGLISH SPORTS PRESENTER

———— •●• ————

Well, I can play in the centre,
on the right, and occasionally
on the left-hand side.

DAVID BECKHAM WHEN ASKED IF IT WOULD BE FAIR
TO DESCRIBE HIM AS A VOLATILE PLAYER

WHISTLE-STOP TOURS

What whistles and licks
Alex Ferguson's arse?
A Premiership referee.

ANONYMOUS

I'm trying to be careful what I say, but the referee was useless.

DAVID JONES, ENGLISH FOOTBALLER AND MANAGER

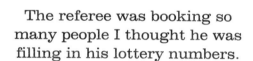

The referee was booking so many people I thought he was filling in his lottery numbers.

IAN WRIGHT, ENGLISH FOOTBALLER AND PUNDIT

Football is a game with 22 players, two linesmen and 20,000 referees.

BOB MONKHOUSE, ENGLISH COMEDIAN

After the match an official
asked for two of my players
to take a dope test. I offered
them the referee.

TOMMY DOCHERTY

I used to play football in my
youth but then my eyes went
bad so I became a referee.

ERIC MORECAMBE, ENGLISH COMEDIAN

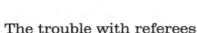

The trouble with referees
is that they just don't
care which side wins.

TOM CANTERBURY

I've seen harder tackles in the pie queue at half-time than the ones punished in games.

GEORGE FULSTON, FOOTBALL CLUB CHAIRMAN,
ON OVERLY STRICT REFEREES

I never comment on referees
and I'm not going to break the
habit of a lifetime for that prat.

RON ATKINSON, 'BIG RON', ENGLISH FOOTBALLER AND MANAGER

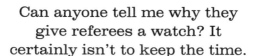

Can anyone tell me why they
give referees a watch? It
certainly isn't to keep the time.

ALEX FERGUSON, SCOTTISH FOOTBALLER AND MANAGER

If the fourth official had done his
job it wouldn't have happened, but
I don't want to blame anyone.

JOHN ALDRIDGE, IRISH FOOTBALLER AND MANAGER

FANNING THE FLAMES

Every fan you ask
will say he wants
to see lively, open
football, but what the
fan really wants to
see is his team win.

DENNIS HILL-WOOD, FOOTBALL CLUB CHAIRMAN

Why do Arsenal
fans smell?
So the blind can
hate them as well.

JOE LYNAM, IRISH JOURNALIST

England have the best fans in
the world, and Scotland's ones
are also second to none.

KEVIN KEEGAN, ENGLISH FOOTBALLER AND MANAGER

The Shit Hits The Fan

NEWS OF THE WORLD HEADLINE AFTER ERIC CANTONA'S
FAMOUS ATTACK ON A CRYSTAL PALACE SUPPORTER IN 1995

The fans like to see Balde
wear his shirt on his sleeve.

KENNY DALGLISH, SCOTTISH FOOTBALLER AND MANAGER

CREATIVE MATHEMATICS

I've got 14 bookings
this season, eight of
which were my fault
and seven of which
were disputable.

PAUL GASCOIGNE, ENGLISH FOOTBALLER

Argentina are the second best
team in the world, and there's
no higher praise than that.

KEVIN KEEGAN

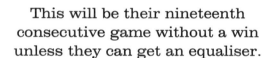

This will be their nineteenth
consecutive game without a win
unless they can get an equaliser.

ALAN GREEN, IRISH SPORTS COMMENTATOR

Kevin Keegan and I have 63
international caps between
us. He has 63 of them.

CRAIG BROWN

Ireland will give 99 per cent
– everything they've got.

MARK LAWRENSON, IRISH FOOTBALLER AND PUNDIT

———— •••• ————

Southampton have beaten
Brighton by three goals to 1.
That's a repeat of last year's result
when Southampton won 5–1.

DES LYNAM, IRISH TELEVISION AND RADIO PRESENTER

———— •••• ————

They've won 66 games, and
scored in all of them.

BRIAN MOORE, ENGLISH SPORTS COMMENTATOR
AND TELEVISION PRESENTER

Ritchie has now scored 11
goals, exactly double the
number he got last season.

ALAN FURRY

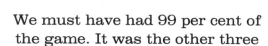

We must have had 99 per cent of
the game. It was the other three
per cent that cost us the match.

RUUD GULLIT, DUTCH FOOTBALLER AND MANAGER

One year I played for 15 months.

FRANZ BECKENBAUER, GERMAN FOOTBALLER AND MANAGER

The last time Ireland played
England we beat them one–all.

JIM SHERIDAN, IRISH FILM DIRECTOR

———•••———

They had a dozen corners,
maybe 12, I'm guessing.

CRAIG BROWN, SCOTTISH FOOTBALLER AND MANAGER

———•••———

Mirandinha will have more
shots this afternoon than
both sides put together.

MALCOLM MCDONALD, ENGLISH FOOTBALLER

Meade had a hat-trick.
He scored two goals.

RICHARD WHITMORE, ENGLISH BROADCASTER

If you had to name one
person to blame it would
have to be the players.

THEO FOLEY, IRISH FOOTBALLER AND MANAGER

The first 90 minutes of a football
match are the most important.

BOBBY ROBSON, ENGLISH FOOTBALLER AND MANAGER

A BLOOD SPORT

I'm not happy with our tackling, boys. We keep hurting them, but they keep getting up.

JIMMY MURPHY, WELSH FOOTBALLER AND MANAGER

If he fouls you he normally picks
you up, but the referee doesn't
see what he picks you up by.

RYAN GIGGS, WELSH FOOTBALLER, ON DENNIS WISE

I'm always telling Craig Russell
to run at players with the ball,
and he does it. Do you know
why? Because I tell him I'll
break his legs if he doesn't.

MICK BUXTON, SUNDERLAND MANAGER

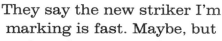

They say the new striker I'm
marking is fast. Maybe, but
how fast can he limp?

MICK MCCARTHY, IRISH FOOTBALLER AND MANAGER

If his car broke down and I saw him thumbing a lift I wouldn't pick him up. I'd run him over.

BRIAN CLOUGH, ENGLISH FOOTBALLER AND MANAGER, ON PETER TAYLOR, FOLLOWING A ROW WITH HIM

•••

The Liverpool theme song is 'You'll Never Walk Alone'. The Wimbledon one is 'You'll Never Walk Again'.

TOMMY DOCHERTY

•••

In football it is widely acknowledged that if both sides agree to cheat, then cheating is fair.

C. B. FRY, ENGLISH FOOTBALLER AND CRICKETER

It's not fair to say
that Lee Bowyer is
racist; he'd stamp
on anyone's head.

RODNEY MARSH, ENGLISH FOOTBALLER

When David Webb was manager
of Bournemouth he never thought
training was any good unless
there'd been a punch-up.

HARRY REDKNAPP, ENGLISH FOOTBALLER AND MANAGER

———— •❂• ————

Norman Hunter doesn't so much
tackle players as break them
down for re-sale as scrap.

JULIE WELCH, BRITISH SPORTSWRITER

———— •❂• ————

The rules of soccer are simple.
If it moves, kick it. If it
doesn't, kick it until it does.

PHIL WOOSNAM, WELSH FOOTBALLER AND COMMISSIONER
OF THE NORTH AMERICAN SOCCER LEAGUE

It's very unfair to ask any man
to stand in a human wall during
a soccer match. A high-speed
leather ball hitting you squarely
in the pleasure centre could raise
your voice by 100 octaves and
have you talking like Quasimodo
for the rest of your life.

PAT INGOLDSBY, IRISH POET

—•••—

Referees at Celtic–Rangers
matches always have a hard
time. One particular unfortunate,
officiating at his first fixture,
was checking in with the team
managers before the kick-off.
'Well that seems to be everything,'
said the Rangers boss, 'Now if
you'd just like to give us the
name and address of your next
of kin, we can start the match.'

EDWARD PHILLIPS

TIME'S WINGED CHARIOT

As with every
young player, he's
only eighteen.

ALEX FERGUSON ON DAVID BECKHAM

He had an eternity to play that
ball but he took too long over it.

MARTIN TYLER, ENGLISH FOOTBALL COMMENTATOR

———— •••• ————

Chris Kirkland's future is
definitely in front of him.

ANDY GRAY, SCOTTISH FOOTBALLER AND COMMENTATOR

———— •••• ————

The ageless Dennis Wise,
now in his thirties.

MARTIN TYLER

Michael Owen isn't a natural goal-scorer yet. That takes time.

GLENN HODDLE, ENGLISH FOOTBALLER AND MANAGER

We're a young side that will only get younger.

PAUL HART, ENGLISH FOOTBALLER AND MANAGER, ON NOTTINGHAM FOREST

My parents have been there for me ever since I was about seven.

DAVID BECKHAM

A SAFE PAIR OF HANDS?

You have to remember
that a goalkeeper is a
goalkeeper because he
can't play football.

RUUD GULLIT

Neville Southall was a big, daft
goalie. He had a sponsored car
but he couldn't drive. And he once
turned up at Wembley wearing
his suit and a pair of flip-flops.

ANDY GRAY

———————•●•———————

The Pope was a soccer
goalkeeper in his youth. Even
as a young man he tried to
stop people from scoring.

CONAN O'BRIEN, AMERICAN TV HOST AND COMEDIAN

———————•●•———————

David Icke says he's here to
save the world. Well he saved
bugger all when he played
in goal for Coventry.

JASPER CARROTT, ENGLISH COMEDIAN

Dino Zoff is all right with the
high balls, but with the low ones
he goes down in instalments.

IAN ST JOHN, SCOTTISH FOOTBALLER, ON THE ITALIAN GOALKEEPER

———•◦•———

He hasn't made any saves
you wouldn't have expected
him not to make.

LIAM BRADY, IRISH FOOTBALLER AND ASSISTANT MANAGER

———•◦•———

Dutch goalkeepers are protected
to a ridiculous extent. The
only time they're in danger of
physical contact is when they
go into a red-light district.

BRIAN CLOUGH

Poor Scott Carson. Just two more hands and another chest and he would have saved it.

JIMMY GREAVES, ENGLISH FOOTBALLER AND TV PUNDIT, ON ONE OF THE GOALS THAT PUT ENGLAND OUT OF EURO 2008

That would have been a goal if
the goalkeeper hadn't saved it.

KEVIN KEEGAN

The most vulnerable area for
goalies is between their legs.

ANDY GRAY

It's not nice going into the
supermarket and the woman at the
till is thinking, 'Dodgy keeper'.

DAVID JAMES, ENGLISH GOALKEEPER

IDENTITY CRISES

Hoddle hasn't been the
Hoddle we know, and
neither has Robson.

RON GREENWOOD, ENGLISH FOOTBALLER AND MANAGER

Who should be there at the far post
but yours truly, Alan Shearer.

COLIN HENDRY, SCOTTISH FOOTBALLER

There's no way Ryan Giggs
is another George Best. He's
another Ryan Giggs.

DENIS LAW, SCOTTISH FOOTBALLER

When it comes to the David
Beckhams of the world, this guy's
up there with Roberto Carlos.

DUNCAN MCKENZIE, ENGLISH FOOTBALLER

If that lad makes a First
Division footballer, my
name is Mao Tse-tung.

TOMMY DOCHERTY ON DWIGHT YORKE

———————•●•———————

The last player to score a hat-
trick in the FA Cup Final
was Stan Mortenson. He
even had a final named after
him, the Matthews Final.

LAWRIE MCMENEMY, ENGLISH MANAGER

———————•●•———————

Duncan Ferguson became a legend
before he became a player.

JOE ROYLE, ENGLISH FOOTBALLER AND MANAGER

INTERNATIONAL DUTY

Other nations
have history. We
have football.

ONDINO VIERA, URUGUAYAN MANAGER

The Brazilians aren't as good as they used to be, or as they are now.

KENNY DALGLISH, SCOTTISH FOOTBALLER AND MANAGER

———— •••• ————

I'd love to play for one of those Italian teams like Barcelona.

MARK DRAPER, ENGLISH FOOTBALLER

———— •••• ————

If you have a fortnight's holiday in Dublin you qualify to play for the national side.

MIKE ENGLAND, WELSH FOOTBALLER AND MANAGER

I've just named the team I
would like to represent Wales
in the next World Cup: Brazil.

BOBBY GOULD, ENGLISH FOOTBALLER AND
MANAGER OF THE WELSH NATIONAL TEAM

The Koreans were quicker
in terms of speed.

MARK LAWRENSON

The English football team –
brilliant on paper, shit on grass.

ARTHUR SMITH, ENGLISH COMEDIAN AND WRITER

Playing with wingers is more
effective against European
sides like Brazil than
English sides like Wales.

RON GREENWOOD

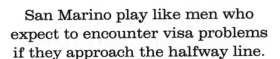

To play Holland you have
to play the Dutch.

RUUD GULLIT

San Marino play like men who
expect to encounter visa problems
if they approach the halfway line.

TOM HUMPHRIES, IRISH SPORTS JOURNALIST

The Croatians don't play well without the ball.

BARRY VENISON, ENGLISH FOOTBALLER AND PUNDIT

The tune began changing when
the Peruvians, a goal down,
suddenly revealed an ability to
run faster with the ball than the
Scots could run without it.

CLIVE JAMES, AUSTRALIAN BROADCASTER, ON THE 1978 WORLD CUP

Scotland has the only football
team in the world that
does a lap of disgrace.

BILLY CONNOLLY, SCOTTISH COMEDIAN

'66 was a great year for English
football. Eric Cantona was born.

GRAFFITI

SIX OF THE BEST

When they first
installed all-seater
stadiums everyone
predicted that the fans
wouldn't stand for it.

GEORGE BEST

I used to dream about taking the
ball round the keeper, stopping
it on the line and then getting
down on my hands and knees
and heading it into the net.

GEORGE BEST

———— •●• ————

Bobby Collins was so small
we used to say he was the
only player in the league who
had turn-ups on his shorts.

GEORGE BEST

If Tommy Docherty says
'Good morning' to you,
check the weather.

GEORGE BEST

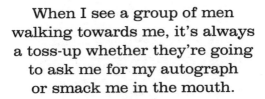

When I see a group of men
walking towards me, it's always
a toss-up whether they're going
to ask me for my autograph
or smack me in the mouth.

GEORGE BEST

Great managers have to be
ugly and swear a lot.

GEORGE BEST

INJURY TIME

I was watching
Germany and I got
up to make a cup
of tea. I bumped
into the telly and
Klinsmann fell over.

FRANK SKINNER, ENGLISH COMEDIAN

Leeds United are having problems with injuries. The players keep recovering.

BILL SHANKLY, SCOTTISH FOOTBALLER AND MANAGER, AT A TIME WHEN LEEDS WERE HAVING A BAD RUN

———●●●———

He's had two cruciates and a broken ankle. That's not easy. Every player attached to the club is praying the boy gets a break.

ALEX FERGUSON ON WES BROWN

My ankle was pointing
towards Hong Kong so
I knew I was in trouble.

ALAN SMITH, ENGLISH FOOTBALLER AND PUNDIT

John Barnes's problem is that
he gets injured appearing
on *A Question of Sport*.

TOMMY DOCHERTY

Then there was the football fan
who sued a Scottish League club
because he was injured while
watching a match. He fell out of
the tree beside the grounds.

JIM MCTAIG

When England go to Turkey
there could be fatalities. Or
even worse, injuries.

PHIL NEAL, ENGLISH FOOTBALLER AND MANAGER

CLUB LIFE

The problems at
Wimbledon seem
to be that the club
has suffered a loss
of complacency.

JOE KINNEAR, IRISH FOOTBALLER AND MANAGER

All Nottingham has is Robin
Hood. And he's dead.

BRYAN ROY, DUTCH FOOTBALLER AND MANAGER,
AFTER HE LEFT NOTTINGHAM FOREST

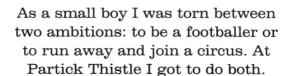

Robert Maxwell's just bought
Brighton and Hove Albion. He's
furious that it's only one club.

TOMMY DOCHERTY

As a small boy I was torn between
two ambitions: to be a footballer or
to run away and join a circus. At
Partick Thistle I got to do both.

ALAN HANSEN, SCOTTISH FOOTBALLER AND PUNDIT

When I played with Barnsley it was a small-town club with a chip on its shoulder. Later I went to Millwall, a club with a chip on both shoulders.

MICK MCCARTHY

———•••———

Southampton is a very well-run football team from Monday to Friday. It's Saturdays we have a problem with.

LAWRIE MCMENEMY

———•••———

Sheffield United couldn't hit a cow's arse with a banjo.

DAVE BASSETT

Watching Manchester City is probably the best laxative you can take.

PHIL NEAL

The two best clubs in London are
Stringfellows and the Hippodrome.

TERRY MCDERMOTT, ENGLISH FOOTBALLER AND MANAGER

The last time Nottingham were
five points ahead of anybody
was in a cricket match.

BRIAN CLOUGH REFERRING TO NOTTINGHAM'S PREMIERSHIP PRIORITY

When you've been given a free
transfer by Rochdale you worry
seriously about your future.

TERRY DOLAN, ENGLISH FOOTBALLER AND MANAGER

When I was at St Mirren's, it was a desolate place. Even the birds woke up coughing.

ALEX FERGUSON

If Everton were playing down at the bottom of my garden, I'd draw the curtains.

BILL SHANKLY

After I joined Celtic I was walking down a street in Glasgow when someone shouted 'Fenian bastard'. I had to go and look it up. Fenian, that is.

MICK MCCARTHY

BOTTLING IT

They say football is a
game of two halves.
Not for me it isn't. I
regularly down eight
or nine pints while
watching a live game
on Sky TV in my local.

ADRIAN BOND

The Scottish football fan's
ability to smuggle drink into
matches makes Papillon
look like an amateur.

PATRICK MURRAY

———◆●◆———

George Best Needed Forty Pints

UNFORTUNATELY AMBIGUOUS NEWSPAPER HEADLINE
AFTER BEST RECEIVED HIS LIVER TRANSPLANT.
THE REFERENCE IS TO BLOOD, NOT BEER

Let me recommend shopping to any young professional football player who feels they're in danger of going off the rails. It has less risk of personal injury than a punch-up outside a nightclub, and you very rarely end up with a hangover.

BRIAN MCCLAIR, SCOTTISH FOOTBALLER AND DIRECTOR

———•••———

Kevin Keegan isn't fit to lace George Best's... whiskeys.

JOHN ROBERTS, BRITISH SPORTSWRITER

———•••———

I pissed it all up against a wall.

BRIAN CLOUGH EXPLAINING HOW DRINK
RUINED HIS MANAGERIAL CAREER

It took a lot of bottle for
Tony Adams to own up
to his drink problem.

IAN WRIGHT

———●●●———

Alcoholism V Communism

BANNER ON DISPLAY DURING THE 1982 WORLD CUP
WHEN SCOTLAND WERE PLAYING RUSSIA

———●●●———

The long ball down the middle is
like pouring beer down the toilet.
It cuts out the middle man.

JACK CHARLTON, ENGLISH FOOTBALLER AND MANAGER

CRYSTAL BALLS

The score is Ipswich nil and Liverpool two. If it stays that way, you've got to fancy Liverpool to win.

PETER JONES, WELSH SPORTS COMMENTATOR

The one thing I didn't expect
is the way we didn't play.

GEORGE GRAHAM, SCOTTISH FOOTBALLER AND MANAGER

———●◆●———

The winner of the Premier
League will come from a
select bunch of one.

PETER KENYON, BRITISH FOOTBALL CLUB CHIEF
EXECUTIVE, AS THE 2006 SEASON STARTED

———●◆●———

I don't think we'll go down. But
then again, the captain of the
Titanic said the same thing.

NEVILLE SOUTHALL, WELSH FOOTBALLER, ON EVERTON'S
CHANCES OF AVOIDING RELEGATION

We didn't underestimate
them. They were just a lot
better than we thought.

BOBBY ROBSON

You've got to believe you're
going to win and I believe
that we'll win the World Cup
until the final whistle blows
and we're knocked out.

PETER SHILTON, ENGLISH FOOTBALLER

If history repeats itself I think we
can expect the same thing again.

TERRY VENABLES, ENGLISH FOOTBALLER AND MANAGER

LET ME REPHRASE THAT

We spoke about it for
a while and out of it
came the fact that he
wouldn't speak about it.

TERRY VENABLES ON A CONVERSATION HE HAD – OR DIDN'T HAVE –
WITH MIDDLESBROUGH CHAIRMAN, STEVE GIBSON, ABOUT HIS FUTURE

The secret of football is to equalise
before the opposition scores.

DANNY BLANCHFLOWER, NORTHERN IRISH FOOTBALLER AND MANAGER

We're now going to Wembley for
live second-half commentary on
the England–Scotland game –
except that it's at Hampden Park.

EAMON ANDREWS, IRISH TELEVISION AND RADIO PRESENTER

The first half was end-to-end
stuff. The second half, in contrast,
was one end to the other.

LOU MACARI, SCOTTISH FOOTBALLER

It was one of those goals
that's invariably a goal.

DENIS LAW

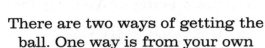

There are two ways of getting the
ball. One way is from your own
players, and that's the only way.

TERRY VENABLES

I watched the game, and I
saw an awful lot of it.

ANDY GRAY

The groin's a little
sore but after the
semi-final I put it to
the back of my head.

MICHAEL HUGHES, NORTHERN IRISH FOOTBALLER

It was a match that could
have gone either way
and very nearly did.

JIM SHERWIN, IRISH SPORTS COMMENTATOR

Achilles tendons are a
pain in the butt.

DAVID O'LEARY, IRISH FOOTBALLER AND MANAGER

There goes Juantorena down
the back straight, opening his
legs and showing his class.

DAVID COLEMAN, ENGLISH SPORTS COMMENTATOR

He sliced the ball when
he had it on a plate.

RON ATKINSON

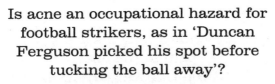

Is acne an occupational hazard for
football strikers, as in 'Duncan
Ferguson picked his spot before
tucking the ball away'?

TOM SHIELDS, SCOTTISH JOURNALIST

You can't take your eye off
this game without seeing
something happen!

HARRY GRATION, ENGLISH BROADCASTER

KISS AND TELL

Alan Shearer is so
dull he once made the
papers for having a
one-in-a-bed romp.

NICK HANCOCK, ENGLISH TELEVISION PRESENTER

Is scoring a goal better than sex? Well it's about five years since I did either, so I must decline to answer that question on grounds of amnesia.

KEN CUNNINGHAM, IRISH FOOTBALLER

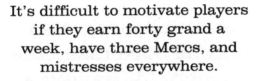

It's difficult to motivate players if they earn forty grand a week, have three Mercs, and mistresses everywhere.

JOE KINNEAR

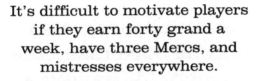

If one of my girls walked in and said, 'Daddy, I'm going out with a footballer,' I'd say, 'No, you were going out with a footballer!'

ANDY GRAY

When I was playing
for Manchester United
I used to go missing a
lot: Miss America, Miss
Uruguay, Miss Peru...

GEORGE BEST

Football and sex are utterly
different. One involves sensuality,
passion, emotion, rushes of
breathtaking, ecstatic excitement
followed by toe-curling orgasmic
pleasure. The other is sex.

JOE O'CONNOR, IRISH NOVELIST

A few more clean sheets and
Sven's problems both on and
off the field would disappear.

BRIAN O'KEEFE

John Bond has blackened my name
with his insinuations about the
private lives of football managers.
Both my wives are upset.

MALCOLM ALLISON, ENGLISH FOOTBALLER AND MANAGER

STRATEGIC SKILLS

There was no point in him coming to team talks. All I used to say was, 'Whenever possible, pass the ball to George.'

MATT BUSBY, SCOTTISH FOOTBALLER AND MANAGER, ON GEORGE BEST

If there's an effective way to kill off the threat of Maradona by marking him, it probably involves putting a white cross over his heart and tethering him to a stake in front of a firing squad. Even then, there would be the fear that he might suddenly drop his shoulder and cause the riflemen to start shooting one another.

HUGH MCILVANNEY, SCOTTISH SPORTSWRITER

———•◉•———

Fail to prepare, prepare to fail.

ROY KEANE, IRISH FOOTBALLER AND MANAGER

———•◉•———

Ally MacLeod thinks tactics are a new kind of peppermint.

BILLY CONNOLLY

If one day the tacticians reached
perfection, the result would
be a nil-all draw... and there'd
be no one there to see it.

PATRICK CRERAND

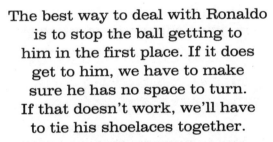

The best way to deal with Ronaldo
is to stop the ball getting to
him in the first place. If it does
get to him, we have to make
sure he has no space to turn.
If that doesn't work, we'll have
to tie his shoelaces together.

JOHN COLLINS, SCOTTISH FOOTBALLER AND MANAGER, ON
SCOTLAND'S WORLD CUP TIE WITH BRAZIL IN 1998

If all else fails, you could wait for
the first corner kick and use his
dreadlocks to tie him to the post.

VINNIE JONES, ENGLISH FOOTBALLER, ON RUUD GULLIT

If you played football on a blackboard, Don Howe would win the World Cup every time.

WILLIE JOHNSTON, SCOTTISH FOOTBALLER

Football isn't just about playing
well. It's about making the
other team play not so well.

ROY PAUL, WELSH FOOTBALLER

It's easy to beat Brazil. You
just stop them getting within
twenty yards from your goal.

BOBBY CHARLTON

Anyone who uses the word
'quintessentially' in a half-time
team talk is talking crap.

MICK MCCARTHY

APPEARANCE ISSUES

So that's what you look like. I've played against you three times and all I've ever seen is your arse.

GRAHAM WILLIAMS, WELSH FOOTBALLER, TO
GEORGE BEST AFTER A BRUISING MATCH

They're calling me Valdarama,
but I feel more like Val Doonican.

ANDY TOWNSEND, IRISH FOOTBALLER AND PUNDIT, AFTER
DYEING HIS HAIR BLONDE FOR THE 1994 WORLD CUP

The image Mark Hughes
conjures up is one that makes
a caricaturist's pen convulse
with joy: legs like tree trunks,
neck muscles that put a pit bull
terrier to shame, elbows flailing
in the penalty box and the guts
of a kamikaze bungee jumper.

CEFIN CAMPBELL

Ryan Giggs: the one with his
eyes too close together, giving
him the aspect of a village idiot.

MARIAN KEYES, IRISH AUTHOR

Ian Rush's hooter is so big he
should have 'Long Vehicle'
stencilled on the back of his head.

DANNY BAKER, ENGLISH COMEDIAN

Bobby Robson's natural expression
is that of a man who fears he
might have left the gas on.

DAVID LACEY, SPORTS JOURNALIST

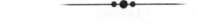

The last time I saw something
like that, it was crawling out of
Sigourney Weaver's stomach.

ALLY MCCOIST, SCOTTISH FOOTBALLER AND MANAGER,
ON SCOTTISH FOOTBALLER DAVID BOWMAN

Kenny Dalglish wasn't that big but he had a huge arse that came down below his knees. That's where he got his strength from.

BRIAN CLOUGH

Mark Hughes is playing better and better, even if he's going grey and starting to look like a pigeon.

GIANLUCA VIALLI, ITALIAN FOOTBALLER

The person who said, 'All men are created equal,' never stepped into a footballers' changing room.

ERIC MORECAMBE

How much further down his head will Bobby Charlton have to part his hair before he faces the fact that he's bald?

CLIVE JAMES

THE LIFE OF BRIAN

I only ever hit Roy
Keane once. He got
up, so I couldn't have
hit him very hard.

BRIAN CLOUGH

I've seen big men hide in corridors to avoid him.

MARTIN O'NEILL

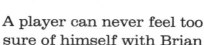

A player can never feel too sure of himself with Brian Clough. That's his secret.

ARCHIE GEMMILL, SCOTTISH FOOTBALLER

We always discuss everything in detail before deciding that I'm right.

BRIAN CLOUGH ON HIS LOCKER ROOM TEAM TALKS

Very few players have the courage of my convictions.

BRIAN CLOUGH

WINNER TAKES ALL

Winning doesn't
really matter as
long as you win.

VINNIE JONES

Whoever wins today will win the championship no matter who wins.

DENIS LAW

I begrudge Manchester United their success, but I am not inconsistent. I begrudged them their failure too.

TOM HUMPHRIES

It's a no-win game for us, although I suppose we can win by winning.

GARY DOHERTY, IRISH FOOTBALLER

Players win matches but
managers lose them.

LIAM HARNAN, IRISH FOOTBALLER

We know what we need to do now
so I think we'll either win or lose.

IAN RUSH, WELSH FOOTBALLER

We got the winner three minutes
from time, but then they equalised.

IAN McNAIL, BRITISH FOOTBALL COMMENTATOR

Winning isn't the end of the world.

DAVID PLEAT, ENGLISH FOOTBALLER, MANAGER AND COMMENTATOR

— •◦• —

We lost because we didn't win.

RONALDO, BRAZILIAN FOOTBALLER

— •◦• —

For a few minutes it looked
like Wigan would win, but
then the game started.

KEN RONAN

IN A MANNER OF
SPEAKING

Manchester United have
got the bull between
their horns now.

BILLY MCNEILL, SCOTTISH FOOTBALLER AND MANAGER

Not being in the Rumbelows
Cup for these teams won't mean
a row of beans, because that's
only small potatoes to them.

IAN ST JOHN

Celtic have taken this game
by the scruff of the throat.

JOHN GREIG, SCOTTISH FOOTBALLER AND MANAGER

If you don't like the heat
in the dressing room, get
out of the kitchen.

TERRY VENABLES

And tonight we have the added ingredient of Kenny Dalglish not being here.

MARTIN TYLER

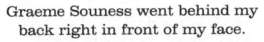

Graeme Souness went behind my back right in front of my face.

CRAIG BELLAMY, WELSH FOOTBALLER

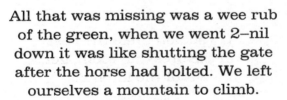

All that was missing was a wee rub of the green, when we went 2–nil down it was like shutting the gate after the horse had bolted. We left ourselves a mountain to climb.

BERT PATON, SCOTTISH FOOTBALLER AND MANAGER, AFTER A DEFEAT

We can only come out
of this game with egg
on our faces, so it's
a real banana skin.

RAY STEWART, SCOTTISH FOOTBALLER, BEFORE
A CRUNCH TIE IN THE SCOTTISH CUP

We could be putting the
hammer in Luton's coffin.

RAY WILKINS, ENGLISH FOOTBALLER AND MANAGER

Liam Brady's been playing inside
Platini's shorts all night.

JIMMY MAGEE, AMERICAN-BORN IRISH SPORTS BROADCASTER

For the benefit of Anglo-
Saxon viewers, I wonder if the
TV sports presenters would
consider using subtitles when
interviewing Kenny Dalglish.

LETTER TO THE LONDON EVENING STANDARD

GOD COMPLEXES

I wouldn't say I was
the best manager in
the business, but I
was in the top one.

BRIAN CLOUGH

Jose Mourinho turned down the position of Pope when he heard it was only an assistant position.

HARRY PEARSON, ENGLISH SPORTS JOURNALIST

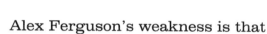

Alex Ferguson's weakness is that he doesn't think he has any.

ARSENE WENGER, FRENCH FOOTBALL MANAGER

The bottom line is that Beardsley is God.

ANDY ROXBURGH, SCOTTISH FOOTBALLER AND MANAGER AFTER PETER BEARDSLEY SCORED SCOTLAND'S WINNING GOAL AGAINST ENGLAND

GOALS, GOALS, GOALS

Norman Whiteside
was more a scorer
of great goals than a
great scorer of goals.

PAUL MCGRATH, IRISH FOOTBALLER

The best thing for them to do is stay at nil–nil until they score a goal.

MARTIN O'NEILL

———— •●• ————

I would have thought that the knowledge that you are going to be leapt on by half a dozen congratulatory but sweaty teammates would be an inducement NOT to score a goal at soccer.

ARTHUR MARSHALL, ENGLISH FOOTBALLER

———— •●• ————

The twenty-first goal was offside.

BRIAN KEIR AFTER HIS UNDER-21 SIDE WON
A MATCH BY 22 GOALS TO NIL

Ryan Giggs did everything
there but score or pass.

TOM TYRELL, SPORTS COMMENTATOR

———•••———

The fools. They've scored too early.

EAMONN SWEENEY, IRISH SPORTS JOURNALIST, ON A GAME OF FOOTBALL
DURING WHICH SLIGO ROVERS F.C. SCORED FIRST AND THEN LOST

———•••———

That's the kind of goal he
normally knocks in in his
sleep with his eyes closed.

ARCHIE MACPHERSON, SCOTTISH FOOTBALL
COMMENTATOR AND AUTHOR

It was the sort of
goal that made
your hair stand on
your shoulders.

NIALL QUINN, IRISH FOOTBALLER AND MANAGER

Apart from their goals,
Norway haven't scored.

TERRY VENABLES

Football is a funny game. Ron
Davies scored 200 league goals
in one season, but the last I
heard of him he was working
somewhere on a building site.

GEORGE BEST

It was particularly pleasing that
our goalscorers scored tonight.

ALEX FERGUSON

We were doing great before
they scored five freak goals.

BERT HEAD, ENGLISH FOOTBALLER AND MANAGER

———•●•———

Our problem is that we've tried
to score too many goals.

GORDON LEE, ENGLISH FOOTBALLER AND MANAGER

———•●•———

After I scored six against
Northampton I hung back for
the last part of the game. I
didn't want to score any more.
It was getting embarrassing.

GEORGE BEST

David Batty is quite prolific,
isn't he? He scores one goal a
season, regular as clockwork.

KENNY DALGLISH

All strikers go through
what they call a glut when
they don't score goals.

MARK LAWRENSON

Woodcock would have scored there
but his shot was just too perfect.

RON ATKINSON

GIRLS WITH BALLS

Show me a man who loves football and nine times out of ten you'll be pointing at a really bad shag.

JO BRAND, ENGLISH COMEDIAN

The woman sits, getting colder
and colder, on a seat getting
harder and harder, watching oafs
getting muddier and muddier.

VIRGINIA GRAHAM, AMERICAN TALK SHOW HOST

———— •●• ————

I'd rather have a guy take
me to a football match and
have a drink afterwards than
go to bed with someone.

SAMANTHA FOX, ENGLISH SINGER AND TELEVISION PERSONALITY

———— •●• ————

I've read David's autobiography
from cover to cover. It's
got some nice pictures.

VICTORIA BECKHAM, ENGLISH SINGER AND
DESIGNER, MARRIED TO DAVID BECKHAM

When men are at a football stadium they're there to watch the game. You could prance half-naked across the pitch and the only response you'll get from the menfolk in the stalls is 'Get off'. Not, you'll notice, 'Get 'em off'.

ANNE MARIE SCANLON, IRISH JOURNALIST AND WRITER

———— ●◦● ————

On the rare occasions he took me out, he talked about nothing but football. By the time I left him, I knew more about it than most managers.

DANIELLE WILSON, THE EX-WIFE OF GRAEME SOUNESS

———— ●◦● ————

So Victoria Beckham got pregnant during the last World Cup. Well it's nice to see David had something on target.

ANGELA MILLER, AMERICAN SINGER-SONGWRITER

A man's sexual fantasy is two lesbians and a donkey making out to the music of *Match of the Day*. A woman's sexual fantasy is a man doing the hoovering now and again.

JO BRAND

SURVIVAL OF THE FITTEST

Ian Rush is perfectly
fit apart from his
physical fitness.

MIKE ENGLAND, WELSH FOOTBALLER AND MANAGER

He's put on weight and I've
lost it, and vice versa.

RONNIE WHELAN, IRISH FOOTBALLER AND MANAGER

———•◆•———

Damien Duff has been known
to suffer from Adhesive
Mattress Syndrome.

BRIAN KERR

———•◆•———

I've introduced something new to
the training. It's called running.

GERRY FRANCIS, ENGLISH FOOTBALLER AND MANAGER,
AFTER HE TOOK OVER AS MANAGER OF SPURS

Pat Crerand is deceptive: he's
slower than you think.

BILL SHANKLY

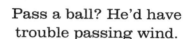

Pass a ball? He'd have
trouble passing wind.

ALF RAMSEY, ENGLISH FOOTBALLER AND MANAGER,
ON DUTCH INTERNATIONAL, PIET FRANSEN

I had to remind the players
that I've had open heart
surgery and there's no way I
can have this every week.

GRAEME SOUNESS AFTER A 4-3 THRILLER BETWEEN
HIS NEWCASTLE TEAM AND MANCHESTER CITY

UNSAVOURY
COMPARISONS

Vinnie Jones is to
fair football what
Count Dracula was to
blood transfusions.

MICHAEL HERD, SCOTTISH FOOTBALLER

If you can imagine spending
five years with an overgrown
child clambering about in your
attic then you'll have a fair idea
of the impact Graeme Souness
has made on Scottish football.

GRAHAM McCOLL, IRISH AUTHOR AND JOURNALIST

Kenny Dalglish was quiet in the
Liverpool team talks until the
players started talking about
conditions. Then he came on like
a Govan shipyard shop steward.

GRAEME SOUNESS

Michael Owen used to be the baby-
faced assassin. Wayne Rooney is
more like the assassin-faced baby.

THE GUARDIAN

If you're a sports channel
that doesn't have football,
you're effectively shovelling
water with a sieve.

ANDY GRAY

Listening to a modem starting up
for ten minutes through a loud
hailer would be soothing compared
to having to endure one of Steve
Staunton's press conferences.
People have been known to get
tinnitus of the eyes from reading
his newspaper interviews.

DAVID KENNY, IRISH AUTHOR AND BROADCASTER

What is it that Rangers,
Celtic and a three-pin plug
have in common? They're all
completely useless in Europe.

MICHAEL MUNRO

Trevor Ford used to collect
bookings like autographs.

JOHN CHARLES, WELSH FOOTBALLER, WHO NEVER
RECEIVED A BOOKING IN HIS CAREER

———————•●●•———————

Duncan MacKenzie is like
a beautiful motor car – six
owners, but he's been in the
garage most of the time.

JOHN TOSHACK, WELSH FOOTBALLER AND MANAGER

———————•●●•———————

Trevor Brooking floats
like a butterfly – and
stings like one as well.

BRIAN CLOUGH

BORN TO LOSE

A lot of hard work
went into this defeat.

MALCOLM ALLISON

In 1978, in-between
Manchester City winning two
games in succession, there
had been three Popes.

FRANK SKINNER

Where did it all go wrong for us?
It was quite simple really. At the
back, in midfield and up front.

GEORGE GRAHAM AFTER A 2-NIL DEFEAT
FOR LEEDS AGAINST ASTON VILLA

The FA Cup Final is a great
occasion, but only until ten
minutes to three o'clock. That's
when the players come on
and ruin the whole thing.

DANNY BLANCHFLOWER

We don't use a stopwatch to judge our Golden Goal competition now; we use a calendar.

TOMMY DOCHERTY ON WOLVES FC

* * *

Those who tell you it's tough at the top have never been at the bottom.

JOE HARVEY, WELSH FOOTBALLER AND MANAGER

* * *

A robber recently broke into Sunderland's grounds and stole the entire contents of the trophy room. Police are looking for a man with a red and green carpet.

MICHAEL HARKNESS

For years I thought the club's name was Partick Thistle Nil.

BILLY CONNOLLY

***

My doctor told me I should avoid any excitement so I've started watching Millwall.

LES DAWSON, ENGLISH COMEDIAN

***

If I walked on water, my accusers would say it is because I can't swim.

BERTI VOGTS, GERMAN FOOTBALLER AND MANAGER

The trouble with Freud is that
he never played the Glasgow
Empire on Saturday night after
Rangers and Celtic had both lost.

KEN DODD, ENGLISH COMEDIAN AND ACTOR

———————•●•———————

My local football team are so
bad, every time they get a corner
they do a lap of honour.

BOB MONKHOUSE

———————•●•———————

Some teams are so negative they
should be sponsored by Kodak.

TOMMY DOCHERTY

QUICK ON THE UPTAKE

The first half was
even. The second half
was even worse.

PAT SPILLANE, IRISH SPORTS PUNDIT AND GAELIC FOOTBALLER

When the TV people asked
me if I'd like to play a football
manager in a play, I asked how
long it would take. They told me
about ten days. 'That's about
par for the course,' I replied.

TOMMY DOCHERTY

———— •●• ————

Verbal abuse.

BRIAN MCCLAIR, SCOTTISH FOOTBALLER, AFTER BEING
ASKED WHAT HE'D HAD FREE AS A FOOTBALLER

———— •●• ————

Ask any striker what was the
greatest goal he ever scored
and they'll all give you the
same answer – the next one.

IAN RUSH

The standard of sweet trolleys at the team get-togethers.

PAT NEVIN, SCOTTISH FOOTBALLER, AFTER BEING
ASKED WHAT WAS THE GREATEST IMPROVEMENT IN
SCOTTISH FOOTBALL IN THE PAST TEN YEARS

Aye, Everton.

BILL SHANKLY TO A BARBER WHO ASKED HIM IF HE
WANTED 'ANYTHING OFF THE TOP' IN 1962

———•●●•———

A chap was once trying to get me
to play for his club in America.
'We'll pay you $20,000 this year,'
he said, 'and $30,000 next year.'
'OK,' I replied, 'I'll sign next year.'

GEORGE BEST

———•●●•———

Velocity.

KENNY DALGLISH AS HE DASHED BY A REPORTER WHO HAD
ASKED HIM FOR 'A QUICK WORD' AFTER A MATCH

Could I not have two bullets?

ALEX FERGUSON AFTER BEING ASKED IF HE HAD A BULLET IN A GUN,
WOULD HE USE IT ON ARSENE WENGER OR VICTORIA BECKHAM

You say Tony Hateley's good in the air. Aye, but so was Douglas Bader – and he had two wooden legs.

BILL SHANKLY TO TOMMY DOCHERTY

Fuck off Norway.

PAUL GASCOIGNE TO AN OSLO TV CREW WHEN
THEY ASKED HIM FOR A PRE-MATCH COMMENT AT
WEMBLEY BEFORE A WORLD CUP QUALIFIER

THE MONEY MEN

Kenny Dalglish calls his goals tap-ins until we come to the end of the season and we're talking money.

BOB PAISLEY, ENGLISH FOOTBALLER AND MANAGER

He's a money-grabbing cockroach.
I own two pot-bellied pigs and
they don't yelp as much as him.

VINNIE JONES AFTER BEING SENT OFF FOR FOULING
RUUD GULLIT. HE ALLEGED GULLIT 'DIVED'

•••

Maradona was the highest-
paid handballer in history.

CON HOULIHAN, IRISH SPORTSWRITER

•••

No wonder he met me at the
airport; the taxi fare would have
tipped the club into bankruptcy.

NIALL QUINN ON BEING PICKED UP PERSONALLY BY
FULHAM'S MANAGER, MALCOLM MACDONALD,
WHEN HE FIRST SIGNED FOR THE CLUB

Half a million for Remi Moses? You could get the original Moses for that, and the tablets as well.

TOMMY DOCHERTY

I get on a train and sit in second class and people think, 'Tight bastard, all the money he's got and he sits in second class.' So I think, 'Fuck them,' and I go to first class. And then they say, 'Look at that flash fucking bastard in first class!'

PAUL GASCOIGNE

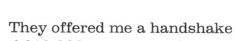

They offered me a handshake of £10,000 to settle amicably. I told them they would have to be a lot more amicable than that.

TOMMY DOCHERTY AFTER BEING RELEASED FROM PRESTON FOOTBALL CLUB

My problem with Paul McGrath was whether to give him appearance money or disappearance money.

RON ATKINSON

The Sheffield United Board
have been honest with me.
When I came here they said
there would be no money and
they've kept their promise.

DAVE BASSETT

—•••—

Premier League football is a multi-
million pound industry with the
aroma of a blocked toilet and the
principles of a knocking shop.

MICHAEL PARKINSON, ENGLISH BROADCASTER AND JOURNALIST

—•••—

Tony Cascarino was the
biggest waste of money since
Madonna's father bought
her a pair of pyjamas.

GORDON MCLAREN

A LITTLE BIT OF IRELAND

The proliferation of
soccer on this island
is about the best
thing that happened
to us since the arrival
of the potato.

CON HOULIHAN

In the Dark Ages BC (Before Charlton) when we were crap, tickets for home games were as abundant on the streets of Dublin as nightclub vouchers midweek.

CONOR O'CALLAGHAN, IRISH POET

———•••———

Stephen Ireland is a riddle inside a mystery wrapped up in an enigma.

GARRY DOYLE, IRISH FOOTBALL JOURNALIST, AFTER THE SOCCER PLAYER WITHDREW FROM IRELAND'S WORLD CUP SQUAD

———•••———

'You'll never beat the Irish' may have become one of football's eternal truths, but there's a very good chance that you're not going to lose to them either.

PAUL HOWARD, IRISH JOURNALIST

People think Ireland is divided
into orange and green. Actually
the predominant colour is
red – Man United red.

EAMONN HOLMES

———————•●●•———————

A few of them moved faster than
they ever did on the pitch!

BRIAN KERR REMINISCING ABOUT A NIGHT HE SPENT IN A
DUBLIN HOTEL WHEN THE IRISH FOOTBALL SQUAD WERE ROUSED
BY A BURGLARY AND A BULLET FIRED INTO THE CEILING

———————•●●•———————

Ever since Italia '90, every
Irishman learned four words
of Italian, 'Olé, olé, olé, olé'.
Except they were Spanish.

NIALL TÓIBÍN, IRISH COMEDIAN AND ACTOR

Jack Charlton's philosophy
of soccer was 'If Plan A
fails, try Plan A'.

MARK LAWRENSON

———◦●●———

Irish sides react as positively to the
tag of favourites as a highly strung
stallion does to first-time blinkers.

ROBERT KITSON, BRITISH SPORTS JOURNALIST

———◦●●———

If Ireland finish with a
draw in winning the game,
that would be fine.

JACK CHARLTON

Danny Blanchflower was a lovely
lad, even though he was Irish.

JOHN CHARLES

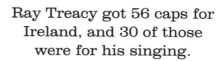

Ray Treacy got 56 caps for
Ireland, and 30 of those
were for his singing.

EAMON DUNPHY, IRISH FOOTBALLER AND SPORTS PUNDIT

Most international studies of
human happiness show that the
average Irish person derives
63 per cent of his or her sense
of wellbeing from watching
England losing football matches.

DECLAN LYNCH, IRISH JOURNALIST AND WRITER

AIMING BELOW THE BELT

Wayne Rooney is
a potato-headed
granny-shagger.

JONATHAN ROSS, ENGLISH TELEVISION AND RADIO PRESENTER

Gordon Strachan's tongue can kill a man at ten paces.

MICK HENNIGAN, ENGLISH FOOTBALLER AND MANAGER

THWACK

I call it 'The Satanic Verses'.

JASON MCATEER, IRISH FOOTBALLER, ON ROY KEANE'S AUTOBIOGRAPHY

———————•••———————

You should only say good
things when somebody leaves.
Robert has gone. Good.

FREDDY SHEPHERD, NEWCASTLE CHAIRMAN, ON THE
FRENCH FOOTBALLER LAUREN ROBERT AFTER
HE LEFT THE CLUB FOR PORTSMOUTH

———————•••———————

Who would have guessed that
behind that arrogant Scots
bastard image there lay an
arrogant Scots bastard?

MIKE TICHER, FOUNDER OF *WHEN SATURDAY COMES*
FOOTBALL MAGAZINE, ON TOMMY DOCHERTY

My second spell at Villa ended
in the summer of 1987 with
the arrival of Graham Taylor.
You could say it resulted
from a clash of personalities.
I had one and he didn't.

ANDY GRAY

I have never met Lee Bowyer,
but everyone I have spoken to
about him says he is a toerag.

TONY CASCARINO, ENGLISH FOOTBALLER

Kenny Dalglish suffers from
constipation of the emotions.

MICHAEL PARKINSON

I went to watch you once
and thought you were
a fat, lazy bastard.

JACK CHARLTON TO TONY CASCARINO BEFORE
SIGNING HIM TO PLAY FOR IRELAND

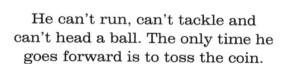

He can't run, can't tackle and
can't head a ball. The only time he
goes forward is to toss the coin.

TOMMY DOCHERTY ON RAY WILKINS

Beckham can't kick with his
left foot. He doesn't score
many goals. He can't head a
ball and he can't tackle. Apart
from that he's all right.

GEORGE BEST

Carlton Palmer covers every blade
of grass on the pitch – mainly
because his first touch is crap.

DAVID JONES

———— •●• ————

If Osvaldo Ardiles had gone to
Arsenal, they'd have had him
marking the opposing keeper.

DANNY BLANCHFLOWER

———— •●• ————

Eric Cantona couldn't
tackle a fish supper.

ALEX FERGUSON

THE WORLD AT THEIR FEET

I was both surprised
and delighted to
take the armband
for both legs.

GARY O'NEILL, IRISH FOOTBALLER

My knees are on their last legs.

PAUL MCGRATH

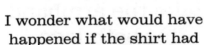

Most players would give their
right arm for his left foot.

MARK LAWRENSON ON JASON WILCOX

I wonder what would have
happened if the shirt had
been on the other foot.

MIKE WALKER

Ian Rush unleashed his left foot
and it hit the back of the net.

MIKE ENGLAND

David Seaman isn't great
when he's got to kick the
ball with his feet.

ALAN HANSEN

He kicked wide of the goal
with great precision.

DES LYNAM

Kevin Kilbane's head is better than his feet. If only he had three heads, one on the end of each leg.

EAMON DUNPHY

My left foot is not one of my best.

SAMMY MCILROY, NORTHERN IRISH FOOTBALLER

I took a whack off my left ankle, but something told me it was my right.

LEE HENDRIE, ENGLISH FOOTBALLER

MEA CULPA

People seem to think that Jack Charlton and myself were influenced by one another. Untrue. I was an arrogant bastard long before I got involved with him.

MICK MCCARTHY

If they'd used video evidence in my day, I'd still be doing time.

GRAEME SOUNESS

———●●—●——

When I joined Rangers I immediately established myself as third-choice left-half. The two guys ahead of me were an amputee and a Catholic.

CRAIG BROWN

I daren't play in a five-a-side at
Anfield because if I collapsed no
one would give me the kiss of life.

GRAEME SOUNESS AFTER OPEN-HEART SURGERY

———•◦•———

We ended up playing football,
and that doesn't suit us.

ALEX MACDONALD, AIRDRIE MANAGER AND SCOTTISH FOOTBALLR

———•◦•———

When I was admitted to the
heart unit, somebody sent me a
Get Well telegram that said, 'We
didn't even know you had one'.

BRIAN CLOUGH

One of the most difficult
tasks I had on match days
was shaking hands with the
opposing manager if I'd lost.

BRIAN CLOUGH

———•●•———

I promised I would take Rotherham
out of the First Division. I did
– into the Second Division.

TOMMY DOCHERTY

———•●•———

One accusation you can't
throw at me is that I've
always done my best.

ALAN SHEARER

KEEPING UP WITH JONES

Not only would I not
sign him, I wouldn't let
him into the ground.

TOMMY DOCHERTY ON VINNIE JONES

I gave a little squeeze. Gently, of course. Gazza didn't squeal. Well, not a lot. I think he tried to but no sound came out.

VINNIE JONES ON THE (IN)FAMOUS TIME HE WAS PHOTOGRAPHED HOLDING ONTO PAUL GASCOIGNE'S 'WOTSITS' DURING A MATCH

Vinnie Jones is as discreet as a scream in a cathedral.

FRANK MCGHEE, ENGLISH SPORTS REPORTER

The Football Association have given me a pat on the back because I've taken violence off the terraces and onto the pitch.

VINNIE JONES

Vinnie Jones has been sentenced
to 120 hours community service,
but this was reduced to 60 hours
on appeal – from the community.

ANGUS DEAYTON, ENGLISH COMEDIAN

If you're going to go over
the top on me you better put
me out of the game or I'll be
coming back for you, either in
five minutes or next season.

VINNIE JONES

Vinnie Jones admits he threw a piece of toast at Gary Lineker. What he didn't say was that it was in the toaster at the time.

TONY BANKS

───●●●───

If you do that again I'll tear your ear off and spit in the hole.

VINNIE JONES TO KENNY DALGLISH FOLLOWING A LATE TACKLE

───●●●───

I always do that to people I like.

VINNIE JONES AFTER BEING ASKED WHY HE BIT A
JOURNALIST ON THE NOSE IN A DUBLIN HOTEL

MAKE YOUR MIND UP

Certain people are
for me, certain
people are pro me.

TERRY VENABLES

When I said they'd scored two
goals what I meant, of course,
was that they only scored one.

GEORGE HAMILTON, SCOTTISH FOOTBALLER

———•●•———

The game is finely balanced,
with Celtic well on top.

JOHN GREIG

———•●•———

We're on the crest of a slump.

JACK CHARLTON

For those of you watching
in black and white, Spurs
are in the all-yellow strip.

JOHN MOTSON, ENGLISH FOOTBALL COMMENTATOR

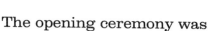

The opening ceremony was
good, although I missed it.

GRAEME LE SAUX, ENGLISH FOOTBALLER

I'm not a believer in luck, but
I do believe you need it.

ALAN BALL, ENGLISH FOOTBALLER AND MANAGER

You can't guarantee anything in football. All you can guarantee is disappointment.

GRAEME SOUNESS

———◦●◦———

I'd rather play in front of a full stadium than an empty crowd.

JOHNNY GILES, IRISH FOOTBALLER AND MANAGER

———◦●◦———

If Glenn Hoddle said one word to his team at half-time, it was concentration and focus.

RON ATKINSON

Our strategy is all-out attack
mixed with caution.

JIM MCLAUGHLIN, NORTHERN IRISH FOOTBALLER AND MANAGER

———•●•———

They're still in the game, and
they're trying to get back into it.

JIMMY HILL, ENGLISH FOOTBALLER, MANAGER AND PRESENTER

———•●•———

Everything in our favour
was against us.

DANNY BLANCHFLOWER

DIFFICULT BODILY MANOEUVRES

Martin O'Neill,
standing, hands on
hips, stroking his chin.

MIKE INGHAM, ENGLISH FOOTBALL COMMENTATOR

With the very last kick
of the game, MacDonald
scored with a header.

ALAN PARRY, ENGLISH SPORTS COMMENTATOR

He caught that with the
outside of his instep.

GEORGE HAMILTON

My legs sort of disappeared
from nowhere.

CHRIS WADDLE, ENGLISH FOOTBALLER

What he's got is legs, which the
other midfielders don't have.

LENNIE LAWRENCE, ENGLISH FOOTBALL MANAGER

We have to roll up our sleeves
and get our knees dirty.

HOWARD WILKINSON

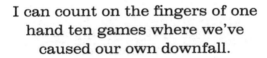

I can count on the fingers of one
hand ten games where we've
caused our own downfall.

JOE KINNEAR

In the last ten minutes of
the match I was breathing
out of my arse.

CLINTON MORRISON, IRISH FOOTBALLER

Here at Old Trafford they reckon
Bestie had double-jointed ankles.

ALEX FERGUSON ON GEORGE BEST

Celtic manager Davie Hay has a
fresh pair of legs up his sleeve.

JOHN GREIG

That's not the type of header
you want to see your defender
make with his hand.

RON ATKINSON

THE BOARDROOM BOYS

John Cobbold's idea
of a boardroom crisis
was when they ran
short of white wine.

BOBBY ROBSON ON IPSWICH CHAIRMAN JOHN COBBOLD

I'm out at the moment, but should
you be the chairman of Barcelona,
AC Milan or Real Madrid, I'll
get straight back to you.

JOE KINNEAR'S ANSWERPHONE MESSAGE

FIFA stands for Forget Irish
Football Altogether.

MICK MCCARTHY

The ideal board of directors
should be made up of three
men: two dead and one dying.

TOMMY DOCHERTY

If you dropped the FIFA crowd
into the ocean, they wouldn't be
able to decide if it was wet or not.

JAKE DUNCAN

• ● •

I'm drinking from a cup today.
I'd prefer a mug, but they're
all in the boardroom.

TOMMY DOCHERTY

• ● •

When the FA get into their
stride they make the Mafia look
like kindergarten material.

BRIAN CLOUGH

PRESS GANGED

There's a place for the press but they haven't dug it yet.

TOMMY DOCHERTY

I sometimes think I must be
the only person in Britain
who has featured on the front,
centre and back pages of a daily
newspaper – all on the same day.

GEORGE BEST

———— •●• ————

If Vinnie Jones hadn't existed,
The Sun would have invented him.

DAVE BASSETT

———— •●• ————

I have told my players never
to believe what I say about
them in the papers.

GRAHAM TAYLOR, ENGLISH FOOTBALLER, MANAGER AND PUNDIT

Mick McCarthy breaks
into a rash if he's
within thirty yards
of an NUJ card.

TOM HUMPHRIES ON IRELAND MANAGER MICK MCCARTHY

THE

FOOTBALL

LOVER'S
COMPANION

Johnny Morgan

THE FOOTBALL LOVER'S COMPANION

Johnny Morgan

£9.99
Hardback
ISBN: 978-1-84953-175-7

*There's no in between – you're either
good or bad. We were in between.*
Gary Lineker on England

When the final whistle blows and you've finished
shouting at the ref, relax with this Premiership-
level miscellany of quotes, jokes, trivia and enough
football-inspired fun to have you rolling on the
ground – even when you're not faking an injury!

You Know You're a

Football Fanatic

When...

Ben Fraser

YOU KNOW'RE A FOOTBALL FANATIC WHEN...

Ben Fraser

£4.99
Hardback
ISBN: 978-1-84953-046-0

You know you're a football fanatic when...

... your mobile ringtone sounds suspiciously like the theme tune for *Match of the Day*.

... you have your house carpeted in AstroTurf.

If this sounds all too familiar, read on to discover whether you're truly obsessed with the beautiful game or just another armchair supporter.

If you're interested in finding out more about our books, find us on Facebook at **Summersdale Publishers** and follow us on Twitter at **@Summersdale**.

www.summersdale.com